Why Me?

Why Me?

Realizing
My Life is Not a ~~Mistake~~

Annette Craig-Wilson

GLORIOUS WORKS PUBLISHING
UPPER DARBY, PENNSYLVANIA

Copyright © 2022 Annette Craig-Wilson

All rights reserved. This book or any portion thereof may not be reproduced or used in any manner whatsoever without the express written permission of the publisher except for the use of brief quotations in a book review or scholarly journal.

First Printing: 2024

ISBN: 978-1-956196-01-6

Glorious Works Publishing

201 Bywood Ave. #2214

Upper Darby, PA19082
www.gloriousworkspublishing.com

Special discounts are available on bulk purchases. For details, contact publisher at admin@gloriousworkspublishing.com.

Glorious Works Publishing can bring authors to your live events. For more information or to book an event, contact Glorious Works Publishing at admin@gloriousworkspublishing.com or visit our website at www.gloriousworkspublishing.com.

Dedication

I dedicate this book to the memory of my late parents, David L. Craig Sr. and Dorothy E. Craig, and my siblings: Mary Lou, Barbara (deceased), Patricia, David Jr. (deceased), William, Dorothy, Sandra, Connie, Leonard, Melissa, Carolyn, Carl, and Charletha, my husband, Larry Sr., my son Larry II, and my precious granddaughters, Londyn Alise and Paris Maliyah. I have been blessed to have an extensive support system of family and special friends who have encouraged me to write this story to bless others.

I want everyone who has ever felt inferior, picked on, put down, different, unworthy, unloved, isolated, or alone to know they can handle and overcome anything the enemy throws at them. With God, we are more than conquerors; we are victorious. I want everyone, especially young people, to know that God loves them just how they are because He created them in His image. We are His special chosen people, and He has a divine plan and purpose for our lives. God is omnipotent, omniscient, and omnipresent; we don't intimidate, offend, or upset Him by asking why.

God encourages us to ask questions and for wisdom when we need answers or guidance. God is attentive to the questions and prayers of His children, and He always answers us according to His timing, not ours. The problem is that we can't always discern or understand God's answers to our questions. For all the promises of God have been fulfilled in Christ with a resounding "Yes," and "Amen" to the glory of God. We have been anointed, blessed, and chosen to accomplish great and miraculous things for God's divine glory.

TABLE OF CONTENTS

INTRODUCTION 1

CHAPTER 1: THE EARLY YEARS 4
   Bewilderment Stage 5

CHAPTER 2: THE TEEN YEARS 18
   Discovery Stage 19

CHAPTER 3: ADULTHOOD 34
   Acceptance Stage 35

CHAPTER 4: MATURITY 50
   Revelation Stage 51

CHAPTER 5: EVOLUTION 60
   Affirmation Stage 61

CHAPTER 6: NUGGETS FOR THE FUTURE 74
   Progression Stage 75

CHAPTER 7: GROWTH AND NEW OPPORTUNITIES 88
   Self-Examination Stage 89

APPENDIX 1 99

APPENDIX 2 101

MEET THE AUTHOR 104

Introduction

I have always felt different and a little strange as far back as I can remember. I did not feel a sense of belonging, at least not in my large family or with my peers. I did not feel important or like I mattered, and perhaps I did not like myself. After all, there was absolutely nothing spectacular about me. I had short, kinky hair, dark skin, and large eyes. I was typically larger than most girls my age; I was well-endowed with a sizeable butt and full hips.

I was timid and afraid to speak up about anything. I grew up in a time when little children were to be seen and not heard. You did not talk back or interject yourself into a grown-folk conversation without being punished. If you had an opinion, you kept it to yourself. Early in life, I learned how to remain unseen, in the shadows, away from everyone else, from the spotlight and any form of unwanted attention. I often wondered, why me? Why did God make me so different from most other girls I saw and knew? Was my life a dreadful mistake? The word mistake means a departure from what is true, correct, or proper. It also denotes attributes of something completed accidentally or out of stupidity or ignorance. Regardless of the meaning, the word mistake has no positive correlation.

There were so many times growing up that I felt my life had no meaning, and I even thought my family and the world, in general, would be better off without me. I did not feel pretty, smart, or significant in any way. It's difficult to explain, but how can a young girl feel so isolated and alone when people are always around her? If God was real, why didn't he love me, and why didn't he make my life better? Why, God, why?

Chapter 1

The Early Years

"My God, my God, why have you forsaken me?"

Matthew 27:46 (NIV)

Bewilderment Stage

Reminiscing, I remember the unbelievable and most embarrassing thing that happened to me in the first grade, and I felt powerless, helpless, and ashamed. I soiled myself because I was too afraid to raise my hand to ask to go to the restroom. I had to go so badly that I could hardly focus on the teacher's words. I wore a pink lacey dress, white ankle socks, and black shoes. Although I wore a pretty dress, I don't remember feeling cute, unique, or worthy. I felt just the opposite, like I did not measure up. Some classmates called me "dumb" and "big baby" for soiling my clothes. Finally, someone yelled, "pissy girl," and everyone in the class laughed at me. I just wanted to crawl into a hole and disappear forever to avoid everyone. I did not want to live, only to face another day of humiliation tomorrow. Why me?

I did not have much hair as a young girl. Several years ago, I found a black and white photo of my older sisters with my nieces and nephew. My nieces and I resembled little Ethiopian girls because she had no hair, and we wore large old dresses with no shoes. I cannot remember the photo's date; however, I feel pitiful looking at it now. God sent an older cousin, Emma, who would visit my sisters to party and hang out on weekends. She was a guardian angel to me and took a particular interest in me for some reason. Emma would pinch and twist my little hair every weekend to help it grow. She was a special blessing to me, and I owe my hair growth to her tireless efforts of working overtime to do my hair almost every week.

I affectionately refer to her as a mother figure because she always showed me love and attention, which I desperately needed. Honestly, I did not feel equal to the other children or prepared to be in the first-grade class. Perhaps the other children had someone to work with at home on their alphabet, numbers, essential reading, and writing skills before the school year started. Most of the schoolwork seemed foreign to me, which made me afraid and nervous about being picked on and labeled stupid. I wondered, "God, why do I feel like this?" What is wrong with me? Why have I been created the way that I was? What made me feel or think this way in my early developmental years?

My mother had me when she was nearly 40 years old. I often wondered if I was a horrible mistake being the last of ten children. Why me?

I remember my mom taking me to the store in the nearby town of Kenbridge on one occasion. I remember feeling so excited because, for once, I had the opportunity to go with her alone. My mom left me in the car while she went into the back of one of the stores. When I saw a large group of young schoolchildren approaching the locked car, I hid in the back seat because I did not want them to see me. I am not sure why I hid from the children. I didn't think they would hurt me; however, I remember feeling like they would pick on me and call me names because somehow, I was different from them, or at least that is what I thought. I felt ashamed of who I was and how I looked. When my mom came to the car and saw me in the back, hiding as the children passed, she asked why I was hiding. She thought something had happened to me. I hung my head and told her that I did not know. After all, I knew that I could not tell her the truth. Why me?

You see, typically, my mom only took my brother, who was only nine months older than me, with her for some reason. She seemed overly protective of him, which I could not understand as a young child. My mom's special treatment and care for my brother made me feel insignificant, like I was not good enough, and she loved my brother more than me for some reason. It is hard for children to witness other siblings being treated better and given more attention than them. Any time a child perceives that their parent likes another sibling more than them, it only adds to their feelings of self-doubt, hatred, and insignificance.

It was not until years later that my oldest sister revealed the big family secret that my brother and I had different dads. I remember feeling numb and mortified when I first heard the news. I did not love my brother any less or think differently because of this new family revelation. Still, everything made more sense to me now. My mom didn't love my brother more than me; she loved him differently for obvious reasons. I realized my mom was very protective of my brother because she thought she needed to shield him from my dad as a young child. I don't remember anything threatening or harmful ever happening to my brother; however, my mom felt she needed to keep him close and protect him for some reason.

My dad was a strict, loving, and supportive man who could be mean and violent when drinking too much alcohol. My dad used to say, "Always say what you mean and mean what you say," all the time. When he spoke, everyone in the house listened; we did not question him or dare talk back. If you did, you would suffer the consequences. I grew up when it was perfectly legal to spank your children for disobedience with whatever was handy, a shoe, belt, or long narrow switch from a tree. I don't recall violent altercations between my parents. However, my other siblings told us about those challenging and often scary weekends from their youth long ago. I thank God that part of my parents' lives was over before the younger children like me grew up.

Several of my other siblings had a different biological mother; however, we loved and always treated them as part of our immediate family. Family secrets like this can be very damaging. Family secrets can also leave children questioning their self-worth and existence, just like I did growing up. Why me?

I survived the first grade; however, my second-grade teacher told my mom I was not ready for the third grade. She wrote a letter to my mother explaining that I needed to be in a remedial class to better prepare me before going to the next level. I felt horrible and sad to be left behind by my other classmates. Now, I hated myself. I did not like who I was or whom God had created me to be. I was angry at God, my teacher, and everyone else because of what happened to me. Was I slow, mentally challenged, or just stupid? I seemed not to comprehend or process information like the other children in my class. Why me?

By the time I got to third grade, I was diagnosed with dyslexia, which caused me to have trouble speaking, reading, and comprehending. My reading teacher said my condition caused my mind to mix up letters, sounds, and words. The teacher told my mom my mind was thinking faster than I could write or articulate the information aloud. I was smart;

however, my unique condition made it difficult to pronounce words. Sometimes when I was talking or reading, the words would get jumbled up or come out backward for some odd reason. I did not need anything else to make me feel inferior or different. Why me?

I am reminded of Moses's story in the Old Testament because he also had a speech impediment; however, God used him in a mighty way to deliver his people. When God first spoke to Moses out of the burning bush, he called him to deliver his people from captivity in Egypt and Pharaoh's oppression. He told God to pardon him and choose someone else for the assignment because he was slow in speech and tongue. Somehow, Moses thought God had forgotten his speech problem. Moses did not believe that he spoke well enough to boldly and confidently tell Pharaoh to let God's people go.

The Lord did not let him off the hook or allow him to give up on his divine assignment or purpose as a deliverer.

Now, I realize everything I went through, the low self-esteem, the feelings of being inadequate, the self-hatred, and the feelings of loneliness and isolation, God allowed as part of his divine plan for my life. I remember the ugly things the kids used to say and the names they called me: ugly, dark, dumb, poor, and stupid. I would not say a word because I didn't want to be a tattletale or get into trouble by fighting.

Sometimes, the kids in school can be so mean and cruel for no other reason than to hurt you, make you feel inferior to them, and somehow feel better about their empty lives. Trust me; the other children are not better than you. They are insecure; some kids make fun of or put others down to make themselves seem important or better than they are. It is unfortunate. Why Me? Indeed God chose me; he made me different and unique for a reason.

Chapter 2

The Teen Years

How long, Lord? Will you forget me forever?
How long will you hide your face from me?
How long must I wrestle with my thoughts and
day after day have sorrow in my heart?
How long will my enemy triumph over me?
Psalms 13:1-2 (NIV)

Discovery Stage

While in the seventh grade in Mr. Coleman's classroom, I remember everyone had to see the nurse for a routine physical exam. The state-mandated exam was designed to detect spinal cord abnormalities in pre-teens during their growth years. To my surprise, the nurse sent a note to notify my parents that I had an extensive sideways curve of the spine between my shoulder blades called scoliosis. My parents and I regularly visited the Crippled Children Hospital in Richmond, VA, until age 16. At the hospital, I had to undergo a series of spinal x-rays and completed numerous exercises for the specialists.

The doctors monitored the curve in my back to ensure it was not getting any worse as my body approached maturity. This medical condition is visibly undetectable to the naked eye, so none of my classmates knew about my handicap. My scoliosis diagnosis did not cause me pain or discomfort or restrict my physical activities, at least not as a young active child. This scoliosis was another bad thing happening to me in my young mind and another reason to cry out to God. Why, God, why?

I excelled in middle school and high school, despite all the things I felt and went through. I was not one of the popular kids, so I found it easier to keep to myself most of the time. I had developed a few good friendships and was starting to walk in a newfound sense of self-confidence and awareness as a teenager. I was accused of "acting cute" or "trying to be better than others" by some high school girls. I remember one girl asserting, "You think you're better than me just because you make good grades!" Imagine that; I never understood ridiculous comments like that. Why do mean girls say, "I do not like you because you think you are cute?" Sometimes girls do not like you for no apparent reason other than they are jealous for some reason. These girls become your haters and motivators because they make you want to work harder to be your best. If they talk about you, give them something worthwhile to share with others. These girls resent that you seem destined for bigger and better things in life, and they know that you will be somebody extraordinary one day.

Sometimes your haters can see something in you or your true God-given potential and light before you do. I have learned that you cannot hide or dim your God-given light because others feel threatened by you or what God has placed within you. If you were to ask the mean girls why they do not like you, they could not articulate or explain their unsubstantiated feelings. I learned to ignore the mean, jealous girls and remained humble and confident. They are not worthy of your precious time, energy, or thoughts. Getting into a physical altercation or verbal confrontation with foolish people is never good. Why me?

While we were growing up, my cousin, Kimmie, would stay with us to take a summer vacation from her inner-city life. She would stay with us and hang out on the weekends; however, unlike us, she did not have to work in the tobacco fields. I loved my cousin, but we all hated that she did not help us work in the fields or do daily household chores. My cousin was a free spirit. She always seemed to have a lot going on, especially getting in fights or confrontations with the other girls living in her apartment building or high school. I admired her outgoing personality and carefree attitude about life. Unlike me, she was not afraid to take chances or speak up if something bothered her or she wanted something. I was happy to see her come and even happier to see her go home at the end of the summer. She always seemed to need so much attention from everyone, which sometimes felt overwhelming.

As a teenager, I used all my energy to focus on my schoolwork and grades. I remember awakening one morning and getting on the bus to take my typical 30-minute ride to my high school. Suddenly, I felt my mouth twist to the left side for no apparent reason. I tried to talk, but my mouth kept sliding to the left side. I was afraid because I did not know what was going on. The other students in my classes and my teachers kept asking me what was wrong with my mouth throughout the day. I did not know what was wrong because I did not feel sick.

When I got home, I showed my mom my twisted mouth, and she said I probably had a slight stroke. What! Imagine hearing this type of comment as a teenager. I was horrified. She asked if my head was hurting or my heart was beating fast. I told her, "No, it happened on the way to school for some reason."

She took me to the doctor, who said everything looked good. The local county doctor could not explain my health condition or what caused my mouth to be slightly deformed. He said it was probably Bell's palsy, not a stroke.

Bell's palsy is a type of facial paralysis caused by damage or trauma of the seventh cranial or facial nerve. The nerve moves through the fallopian canal, a narrow, bony canal in the skull beneath the ear's lobe, then moves to the side of the face. This condition results in the inability to control the affected facial nerves and muscles. The cranial nerve manages facial expressions such as eye blinking, closing, smiling, frowning, and carrying nerve impulses to the tear and salivary glands. This nerve is also vital for hearing because it transports nerve impulses to the stapes muscles, a small bone in the middle ear, and nerve impulses from the tongue to the brain. I had to research Bell's palsy to understand why it was.

The symptoms of Bell's palsy can vary from mild to severe. There is no specific reason why some people get Bell's palsy, and others do not; however, currently, there is no known cure. I suffered from this facial paralysis and deformity for nearly a month before my mouth returned to normal. I was embarrassed to talk and would put my hand over my mouth to avoid the weird stares and crazy annoying questions. Some people looked at me like I was strange or had some disease or something. I guess they felt sorry for me. Why me?

I was fortunate because many people with Bell's palsy never regained their normal facial functions. God healed my face and helped me overcome the shame and embarrassment associated with a facial deformity. Honestly, it seemed like my complexion was even more radiant and attractive after

God healed me. At this point in my life, I felt like something was always wrong or unfortunate. Why me?

As much as I tried to avoid a physical confrontation, everything changed in high school when a former childhood friend approached me and asked why I did not like her. When I quickly responded sarcastically, "I just don't like you," she raised her hand to slap me. Before I knew it, we were rolling on the hallway floor, pulling hair, punching, and pushing each other. One of the teachers pulled us apart, and we kept yelling and launching at each other because we wanted to finish the "cat" fight. We were both suspended for five days of suspension for fighting. My teachers were shocked that I had gotten into a physical altercation with another student. I had never been in any disciplinary trouble before.

Honestly, I was disappointed in myself for allowing this young lady to aggravate and push me to the point of fighting. Instead of getting into a fight or heated confrontation, I should have just walked away as I had done many times before. I was fed up, tired of being picked on, and intimidated by mean girls in my school. It's regrettable; however, standing up for myself and fighting, in this case, earned me a false sense of respect from some of the mean girls in school. When I got home, I thought my mom and dad would kill me or, at a minimum, punish me with a physical beating.

To my surprise, my parents said very little other than being shocked and disappointed by my behavior. Dad always told us that if someone hit us first, we had the right to hit them back or defend ourselves by any means necessary. My parents knew that I always had good grades and never got into trouble in school. I remember feeling so relieved, but it was hard being home without having anything to do, mainly since my other siblings were in school. Nevertheless, I could get my school assignments during my suspension to maintain good grades.

Back in junior high school, if a girl had threatened to fight or beat me up, my older brother, by only nine months, would gladly fight for me. On one occasion, a big bully girl who was always in trouble fighting told my brother that she would beat my "black butt" because she did not like me. She was a big muscular girl who probably disliked me because I did not bow down to her or give her money or gifts like many other frightened girls in our school. I usually ignored her and her silly friends. I tried to mind my business in school and avoid trouble for the most part.

On the flip side, my brother took the comment and physical threat to beat me up seriously; he beat the bully girl up after school as if she was another boy. Ultimately, the big bully never repeated another bad thing about me; at least, she did not say it to my face or for my brother to hear. He got suspended for ten days, but he did not care. He was not about to let a big bully, or anyone beat up his younger sister for no reason, especially since I never picked on anyone. There was another memorable fight on the bus ride home. I took the liberty to throw a few punches during an altercation between my brother and neighborhood troublemakers. They were constantly arguing and fighting someone for some crazy reason. The troubled neighborhood family eventually moved to another school district because they claimed everyone was unfairly picking on them. This physical altercation resulted in a ten-day suspension for my brother and other neighborhood troublemakers.

I missed having him fight my battles when I got to high school because he quit after 8th grade. He went to work full-time on the farm and worked on automobiles in his spare time. Today, my brother is a successful self-taught auto mechanic. He works for the U.S. government and travels nationwide, working on military vehicles. He also owns his auto mechanic and repair business. He is a living testament to God's divine favor and blessings. He believed in God and his abilities even when most teachers and other adults called him a troublemaker and declared that he would fail. Instead, he proved all the naysayers wrong by making the most of his God-given gifts and talents. I am proud of my brother and share his powerful testimony with people who feel hopeless because of their limited education.

After one specific senseless fight in high school, we were left with scratches, pulled hair, and tattered clothes. The battle was pointless because it solved nothing. The girl and I stayed mad and did not talk to each other for nearly twenty years after graduation for no reason. Thank God we could speak and reconcile our differences before she died unexpectedly at only 53 years old. Forgiveness is not for the other person; it is for you. Unforgiveness will eat away at you; it will cause you to be held in bondage spiritually, emotionally, and physically. Neither of us could even remember what we were upset about or what caused the bad feelings. Sadly, we missed each other's weddings, our children's births, and many other special events and celebrations due to a meaningless disagreement and "cat" fight.

Life is too short to waste on being upset, angry, or holding unforgiveness and bitterness against others. We all have a "time to be born" and a "time to die"; what matters is what we do with the small dash between birth and death. Take time right now to forgive anyone that may have caused you to hurt, harm, or pain in the past because forgiveness sets you free from the burden of unforgiveness in your heart. It releases you from the person who harmed or wronged you.

Despite all my high school challenges, I became a proud member of the National Honor Society with a B+ grade point average. This achievement was indeed a great accomplishment for me. I felt so pleased when the Honor Society letter went home to my parents. Neither of my parents has education beyond elementary and junior high school. Therefore, they wrestled with appreciating this accomplishment as it was our family's first. My mom shared the news with my siblings. She said, "My baby girl is smart." She had never said anything like that before; I realized my mom was proud of me. Like many people, my siblings and I did not grow up in a household where everyone openly confessed their love for one another. Although we did not verbalize the words, we knew our parents loved us, and we loved each other.

Today, I would not trade anything for my large family and their children. I did not realize how blessed I was to grow up in a large family where we never had all we wanted; however, we had all the bare necessities to survive. We always had a pleasant, modest home to live in, homegrown meats and vegetables to eat, and gently worn clothes and shoes that we often had to share. The truth is that I was not smart at all; I just studied a great deal and worked extra hard to get good grades. Contrary to what many people thought, good grades took work. I had to work extra hard to prove I was intelligent, significant, and just as good as everyone else. Why me?

I remember winning a particular essay contest about Rural Electrification for the local electrical company in high school. My government teacher, Ms. Jones, encouraged me to enter the contest. Many students disliked Mrs. Jones because she was a very strict educator. She had a no-nonsense teaching style and would put you out of her class if you were not paying attention or misbehaving. I liked Ms. Jones because she quickly recognized and rewarded hard work and accomplishments. She was always very supportive and encouraging to me. I was so excited to win the contest; I had never won any competition. I was awarded an all-expenses-paid trip to Washington, DC, in the summer of my junior year of high school.

After winning this contest, one of my childhood friends, since the second grade, became so jealous that she stopped talking to me. She told my sister I thought I was special because I had won a "stupid" contest. Her comments and behavior shocked and hurt me because I felt she would be happier than anyone else in my high school because of our long-term friendship and history. I remained gracious and cordial to her; however, our friendship was never the same due to the incident. Why me?

No matter what life throws at us, we cannot become discouraged to the point that we want to give up. God is faithful. He will never start something and not finish it. Therefore, we must have faith in God, believing He will complete what He began in our lives. These Galatians, Philippians, and Isaiah scriptures remind me that God is faithful; we can trust his Word and promises. God's Word will never return to him empty; it will accomplish what he desires and achieve its purpose.

Let us not become weary in doing good, for at the proper time we will reap a harvest if we do not give up.

Galatians 6:9 (NIV)

Being confident of this, that He who began a good work in you will carry it on to completion until the day of Christ Jesus.

Philippians 1:6 (NIV)

So is my Word that goes
Out from my mouth:
It will not return to me empty, but
will accomplish
what I desire and achieve the
purpose for which I sent it.

Isaiah 55:11 (NIV)

Chapter 3

Adulthood

I call out to the Lord, and He answers me from His Holy Mountain.

Psalm 3:4 (NIV)

Acceptance Stage

As I prepared for life after graduation, I remember talking to my high school guidance counselor, an older white lady named Mrs. Moore. I remember her suggesting a trade school or community college versus a more prominent university due to my low college entry test score. Mrs. Moore made assumptions about my intellectual abilities and potential because my parents had limited education, and none of my older siblings had gone to college. I remember thinking that Mrs. Moore did not know me, and she took the time to sit and talk to me or understand what I wanted to accomplish in life. Mrs. Moore was from the older biased school of thought. She tended to classify minority students as less than the Caucasian students in our high school.

My scholastic aptitude test (SAT) scores were lower than the national average for college-bound newcomers. Consequently, my guidance counselor assumed I would fail in a more prominent university with supposedly more competent people than me. I refused to accept the egregious comments from my counselor because I knew deep in my heart that I could be successful if given the opportunity. Although her negative comments hurt me, I remember thinking I would prove her and that stupid SAT wrong. In my opinion, the entire SAT testing process is culturally biased since it does not reflect historical events and facts about people of color before slavery. Why me?

Well, I did it. I finished my last year of school with a B+ average and graduated tenth in my senior class of 1984. Never let anyone stop or limit you with their negative comments and opinions. God has already equipped you with everything you need to succeed in life. Before graduation, I received acceptance letters from Old Dominion University (ODU) in Norfolk, VA, and a few other universities. I was allowed to ODU on a probationary basis to see if I could perform as well as the other first-year students in college, given my relatively low SAT scores. This college acceptance letter was a significant milestone and accomplishment because I would be the first person in my family to attend college after high school.

My family grappled with me going away to college since most of them finished high school and went straight to work in one of the local manufacturing factories in the area. I knew they were proud of my accomplishments up to this point; however, they were skeptical because they were unsure if I could survive away from home alone for an extended period. I remember overhearing one of my sisters say, "She will be back home in no time." That statement hurt my feelings, but I never said anything. I just pretended that I did not hear the comment. I remember thinking it would be a cold day in hell before I returned home as a college dropout or failure. Why me?

When I left home for college the weekend before fall classes started, I remember naively thinking that everything would be great; I would be pushed out of my comfort zone and meet all kinds of new and exciting people. To my surprise, I entered a big cold dormitory full of loud excited teenagers with many personal supplies, clothes, and stuff for their dorm rooms. I felt sad and unprepared because I had only a suitcase and a small throw for my bed. I was so excited and in a big hurry to pack for college; I neglected to read all the essential instructions about what critical supplies to take to live in the dormitory on campus. I was not thinking and did not adequately plan for my new college experience. Why me?

I felt unprepared and like an outcast compared to my peers checking into the dormitory. I went to the front desk to use the phone to call my older brother, Ron, who lived in Virginia Beach, about 25 minutes away. I told him to help because I needed supplies, a blanket, a pillow, and an alarm clock for my dorm room. He came to my rescue and took me to the local Ross store to get what I needed. He was a lifesaver. I could not fathom what I would have done without him because I had minimal funds before receiving my work-study paycheck. My new roommate had not arrived, so I was alone in the large dorm room. The room's furnishings included two naked twin beds with extra-long twin mattresses, two dressers, two lamps, and two large wood desks with two swivel chairs. There were no pictures or comforts of home, so the larger dorm room was cold and uninviting.

When my new roommate arrived the next day, imagine my surprise when I saw that she was a homey-looking white girl. I can still remember the look on her face as she turned her dorm room key and opened the door to find me sitting on my bed reading a magazine. Her name was Lizzy, and she was from a small town in the upper-western part of Virginia. Lizzy's face showed her shock and disbelief as she came to grips with the idea of sharing a dorm room with a black girl. We exchanged pleasant greetings, names, and the townships where we lived. We were friendly and cordial because we were both in unfamiliar territory and forced to live with someone different than us that we did not know.

I am confident Lizzy slept with one eye open because she seemed apprehensive and unsure about living in a room with a person of color. I was also a little frightened because of all the horrible things I had seen and heard about intolerable white people and their mistreatment of black people. I am sure Lizzy was afraid because of all the violent and unlawful acts she had seen about black people on television. She probably thought I would hurt or steal from her. We both had biases and preconceived notions based on misinformation and opinions of our families, friends, and the media, most of which were false and unfounded.

Over time, Lizzy and I got more comfortable with one another to the point that we could talk openly about racial issues and other personal matters. Lizzy told me that the town she grew up in had no people of color, and she had no exposure to any black people growing up in her hometown or school. She admitted that her only information about black people was what she saw on television. I told Lizzy that, contrary to the negative images on television, I was from a low to moderate-income family with two hard-working parents. She would be surprised to know that none of my siblings were killers, incarcerated, or drug dealers. Lizzy asked how I maintained my hair and why it was always so different. I laughed at her naïve questions and innocence. However, she did not know, so I happily answered her ethnic questions to help educate her. While I was hesitant about living with a white girl, Lizzy became the best roommate because she went home almost every weekend, allowing me to enjoy the solitude.

After my first semester, I achieved a 2.9 GPA and was no longer on probationary status. I always knew there was a God; however, it was not until college that I accepted Jesus as my Lord and Savior. Growing up, my oldest sister took me to church with her three children: my nieces and nephew. My nieces were like sisters to me growing up. My biological sisters did not want to hang around with the baby of the family. I remember the old spiritual hymns, Sunday school lessons, church speeches, and plays at her small family-oriented church. I credit my oldest sister, Lou, for helping introduce me to God and helping to shape my early childhood experiences with the church. She did her best to ensure I felt included when planning her children's weekend activities and outings. I am so thankful for her influence when I felt so alone and needed to feel a sense of belonging. Why me?

For the first time in college, everything in my life started to come together and make sense. While away from home, I was alone most of the time, so I spent a great deal of time studying and reading. I picked up a little bible from the library on campus because I longed to know God more intimately. My little, green King James New Testament Bible made it challenging to understand the Greek wording and meaning of the scriptures. I joined a local church near my dorm room and attended a bible study with a few classmates. Why me? I realized that God made me in His image, and He was always with me, so I was not alone. Most importantly, I realized that God loved me just as I was, and it did not matter what anyone else said or thought of me.

This time of acceptance in my life reminds me of Hagar, a young Egyptian handmaiden who lived with Abraham and Sarah. Hagar was treated as an object, a nobody, and used as a surrogate by Sarah and Abraham. Hagar was mistreated so severely by Sarah that she ran away into the wilderness to escape after becoming pregnant. In the wilderness, an angel of the

Lord called Hagar and asked where she came from and where she was going. The angel commanded Hagar to return and submit to Abraham and Sarah, not to be abused but to fulfill her destiny as part of God's plan. Hagar would not return the same way she left; God wanted her to know that her past was not intended to destroy her but make her stronger. Instead, Hagar would return to Sarah and Abraham's home with a covenant promise received directly from God.

After all, Hagar's son's name, Ishmael, means "God hears." The angel of the Lord wanted Hagar to know that God had seen her afflictions and all the horrible things she had endured. God had not forsaken Hagar or her son; he made a solid prophetic promise to Hagar and her son. Although he was not the prophetic child promised to Abraham and Sarah, God promised to make Ishmael the patriarch of many great nations. Hagar called the name of the Lord that spoke to her El Roi, which means "the God who sees me." Hagar had established a personal relationship with God that even Sarah did not have. You see, when Hagar was removed from the control of Abraham and Sarah, she established and developed an intimate relationship with God. This newfound relationship with God, her creator, allowed Hagar to discover her identity and God-given purpose. God saw Hagar and everything she was going through, the good, bad, ugly, great, and small because He never left her side or forsook her. As God was with Hagar, He is also with us, dispensing angels to watch over us. It is good to know that God is always with us no matter what happens.

I graduated from ODU in three and a half years in December 1987. I had no spare time to attend many campus parties, join social groups, or even pledge to my favorite sorority, Alpha Kappa Alpha (AKA). I was determined to achieve the best grades possible to graduate. My main goal was to graduate and find a good-paying job to help me not move back home to the limited opportunities of country living. It was vital for me to finish college in 1987 because it was the year I was supposed to graduate if I had finished high school on time and not been held back in the second grade. College was very challenging and stressful at times. I remember many late nights reading, studying, and writing papers for my classes. Nevertheless, I graduated with a 3.4 GPA and made the Dean's List my last year with all A's. To God, be the glory for saving, keeping, and protecting me all those years as I hated myself and whom He had created me to be in the first place.

In 1987, I also married my childhood sweetheart and my best friend. When I first met my husband-to-be, I did not care for him. I was with my cousin, Kimmie, when he approached us to ask for a dance. He was flirting and dancing around in front of us like he thought he was the main attraction. I told my cousin that I did not like him at all. She said that he was funny and cute. Over time, he grew on me. He would come to my house, pretending to visit my brother to see and talk to me. He was a hard-working country boy who became the unofficial head of his household as a very young man when his dad suddenly and unexpectedly left the family. While he was much older than me, he has always been by my side in one way or another. He encouraged and supported me throughout high school by showing me kindness, love, and affection.

Being the youngest child of a large family, I was not allowed to date until later in high school. We only spent quality time together in my parent's front yard, on long walks, and occasionally going to the drive-in movie theater. We became very close when I went away to college, and he moved to the Tidewater area to work at the shipyard. Many of my most intimate firsts in life occurred with him. Throughout my difficult high school and college years, he was always a confidant and a good friend.

My parents were tobacco farmers (sharecroppers), so they did not have extra money to send me to college. I remember how we used to get up before the sun came up to work in the tobacco fields, and then we would go back to work in the tobacco fields again when we returned home from school. I didn't particularly appreciate working in the hot tobacco fields. Still, we had no choice because this was how my parents made an honest living and supported our large family. I had to pay for college through grants, scholarships, and work-study programs. My special friend sometimes gave me money when I worked up the nerve to ask for financial help. I didn't particularly appreciate asking for financial assistance from others because it made me feel embarrassed, vulnerable, and helpless. I could not have survived high school or college without his encouragement and emotional support. God sent him to be a special blessing to me. Why me?

God wants us to grow and mature and have an attitude of spiritual excellence. We cannot make it apart from God; however, He will send special guardian angels to help us along our spiritual journey. We must forget what lies behind the hurt, pain, shame, and horrible experiences from our past, renew our minds, and reach for what lies ahead to grow spiritually.

Therefore, I urge you, brothers and sisters,

in view of God's mercy

to offer your bodies as a living

sacrifice, holy and pleasing to God—

this is your true and proper worship.

Do not conform to the pattern of this world,

but be transformed by the

renewing of your mind.

Then you will be able to test and approve what

God's will is—His good, pleasing and perfect

will.

Romans 12:1-2 (NIV)

Chapter 4

Maturity

*Now to Him who is able to do immeasurably more than all we ask or imagine,
according to His power that is at work within us, to Him be glory in the church
and in Christ Jesus throughout all generations, forever and ever! Amen.
Ephesians 3:20-21 (NIV)*

Revelation Stage

God had a particular plan for my life and wanted to use me for his glory, not mine. He knew my story would be a testimony to other young people who might feel the way I did growing up and think things would never get any better for them. Someone may even be questioning their very existence. Hopefully, my story inspires others to pursue their dreams, keep pushing forward, and turn their negatives into positives to shame the devil and prove the naysayers wrong.

GOD DID FOR ME whatever I could not accomplish because I was too afraid and weak due to my human frailties. God fought my battles when I could not fight for myself. God covered, blessed, and protected me, even when I did not understand who God was or what He was doing in my life since my birth. God loved me unconditionally and assured me that I was unique and special. God helped me understand that I was made fearfully and wonderfully, perfect in his sight according to his divine plan. Even before I was formed in my mother's womb, God knew me and ordained every aspect of my life. For the first time, I realized that my life was not a horrible mistake; it was all part of God's divine plan.

Today, my question is no longer, "Why me?" The question becomes, "Why not me?" Reminiscing on my past, I realize that everything, the good, bad, ugly, tragic, and life-changing, was part of God's plan for my life and his glory, not mine. Christ came to save a poor little country girl like me. He paid the ultimate price with his life for my salvation and freedom. Christ paid a debt he did not owe, so now we all owe a debt we could never repay. I am thankful for my life and all that I went through. Everything I endured helped mold and shape me into the Christian woman, wife, mother, grandmother, sister, daughter, friend, author, business leader, and business owner I am today. If you ever asked yourself, "why me," my answer is, "why not you?" Even today, this simple little prayer helps me whenever I feel inadequate, unworthy, unloved, or alone.

Father God,

Your Word tells me I am saved by your grace and filled with the Holy Spirit.

You are loving, kind, good, gentle, merciful, patient, and gracious.

You are all these things for me, so when I feel unworthy,

help me stop looking at and comparing myself to others

and fix my eyes and thoughts on you.

Through you, Father God,

I will recognize and acknowledge my true worth and your divine plan for my life.

Search me daily and remove anything unlike you, create a clean heart, and renew a right spirit within me for your glory.

Help me not to doubt or operate with a spirit of fear but to function with power, love, and a sound mind.

Father God, thank you for your protection, divine favor, and unconditional love toward me, even when I did not love myself. In Jesus' Name, Amen!

God is with Us

There is Someone

Who will share

Our burdens and

our sorrows,

And He will never

leave us all alone.

He'll comfort us

Through all of our

tomorrows Because He

made us And we are his

own.

(Author Unknown)

This poem is one that I have kept and repeatedly read through the years to remind me that God is with me. He shares all my burdens and sorrows, no matter what I am going through. In Psalm 46:1, David tells us that God is our refuge and strength, an ever-present help in trouble.

My favorite scripture is from the Book of Proverbs, and it reminds me that if we trust in God, he will direct our paths. God wants to elevate and help us achieve things beyond our wildest imagination. Nevertheless, he asks that we put aside our fears and trust him to lead us.

It takes faith to follow him when you cannot see the destination, where you are going, or what is around the next corner.

Trust in the Lord with all your heart and lean not on your own understanding; in all your ways submit to him, and he will make your paths straight.

Proverbs 3:5-6 (NIV)

I challenge each of you to continue to pray and trust God. He will cover, protect, and keep you no matter your circumstances. God can do exceedingly and abundantly more than you could ever ask or think.

Eyes have not seen, nor have ears heard,

Neither has entered the heart of man,

the things that God has prepared for

them that love him.

1 Corinthians 2:9 (KJV)

Trust me; I am a living witness to God's unconditional love, grace, mercy, and goodness. As you reflect on your life, you will recognize his continued presence, watching over and helping you maneuver through your life's hurt, shame, disappointments, and personal tribulations. God promises never to leave or forsake you, no matter what you are going through, so what makes you ask, "Why me?" For some of you, could it be the negative things people said about you or the "death" comments that people who were supposed to love you spoke over you as a child?

It is not true that words do not hurt. Your spoken words have the power to create and speak things into existence. As a young girl, I remember singing the old nursery rhyme, "Sticks and stones may hurt my bones, but names will never hurt me." Negative and degrading words hurt and penetrate your mind and pierce your soul. Suppose you listen to negative comments long enough. In that case, they will become your reality, and you will start to live and act them out unconsciously. In the Book of Proverbs, we learn that our tongue has the power of life and death; therefore, we must choose our words wisely.

For some of you, that horrific thing that happened to you growing up caused you to feel so much shame and pain that you still cannot forgive the perpetrator. You cannot even talk about the incident to anyone to be set free. Perhaps it is that ugly family secret you do not want anyone else to know about, so you keep it buried deep in your subconscious mind, slowly eating away at you. It is time to release the past pain and forgive, do not do it for others, do it for your self-improvement and spiritual growth. Your past demons and curses no longer have you bound, so let them go. The battle is not yours to fight alone; it is the Lord's. All you need to do is have faith, stand still, and see the salvation of the Lord. God will fight your battles and take care of all your enemies individually. God is the only one that can set you free.

For some, it's the pure rage you feel at your parents or guardians because of how you grew up and the deplorable living conditions you endured. You resent them for not loving you enough or treating you differently from your other siblings because of how you look. You resent them for not making enough money to provide you with all the material things and pleasures that most children your age have to enjoy. You often wonder what you did wrong to end up in your current horrible situation. Maybe your mind is continuously preoccupied with questions to God about "why is this happening" or "why me."

Only the Word of God can provide the truth and answers we seek. God sent his only son to set us free from the bondage of sin and death. The thief comes to steal, kill, and destroy; however, Christ came so that we may have life and life more abundantly.

So, if the Son sets you free, you are truly free.

John 8:36 (NLT)

Ask, and it will be given to you;
Seek, and you will find;
Knock, and the door will be opened to you.

Matthew 7:7 (NIV)

If any of you lacks wisdom,

you should ask God, who

gives generously to all

without finding fault, and it

will be given to you.

James 1:5 (NIV)

Chapter 5
Evolution

God is our refuge and strength, an ever-present help in trouble. Therefore, we will not fear, though the earth give way and the mountains fall into the heart of the sea... Psalm 46:1-2 (NIV)

Affirmation Stage

Looking back, you may shed some tears about your past; however, it did not break or define you. The past is gone, and you are better and stronger today. Most importantly, your tomorrow looks even brighter than yesterday and today. You are more than a conqueror, here to share your remarkable testimony with the world. Our past tragedies and horrific events test our faith, mental stability, and well-being. Still, they did not destroy you, so do not let them cause you to give up on your dreams and God-given purpose in life.

We are all still becoming and evolving into the person God created us to be. We are all good works in process. When we finally arrive, we will probably be ready to die and go on to glory. Take time to forgive yourself for anything God reveals, so you can truly move toward your destiny. Ask God to create a clean heart and renew the right spirit within you. It is time to boldly denounce anger, self-loathing, hatred, depression, jealousy, unforgiveness, doubt, envy, greed, lust, and other small gods which become our idols.

Like Queen Esther in the Old Testament, you have been prepared, groomed, and placed in your exact position or situation for a specific reason or such a time. It may not be to save your entire family, a particular race, or people; however, your divine purpose is no less significant to God. There are no coincidences, and nothing happens by chance with God. He created everything for a specific reason and unique purpose; therefore, I submit that God is calling you, like Queen Ester, for such a time as this.

If you have achieved any measure of success in life, God's grace, mercy, and goodness have blessed you. All your extraordinary experiences and opportunities are not merely for you alone; we have all been blessed to bless others for God's kingdom agenda. You are not a mistake; your life is no accident. God's timing is always perfect. It is your time to stand up, be courageous, and step into your destiny and the purpose for which God has created, ordained, and called you.

In the scriptures, Queen Esther spent three days fasting and praying about her momentous assignment. Going before the King without being summoned could have meant her death. When it was time for Queen Esther to go and speak to the King, she took her time and was deliberate and purposeful with her words and message. Queen Esther asked the King to save her life and the lives of her people. The King listened to her earnest request and was upset about the plot to kill the Jews. He ordered death for the man who would mandate and carry out such an evil conspiracy.

We must have the same passion, patience, confidence, and boldness that Queen Esther had to come before the King to plea for the life of her Jewish people. God wants us to advance His kingdom on earth, just like He used Queen Esther and others before us. He may not use us if we are filled with unrighteous mess, like unforgiveness, pride, malice, and evil motives. The Bible tells us to take a good long look at what is happening in our hearts before we partake in the Lord's Supper.

We are to examine ourselves as we eat the bread representing Christ's body, and drink of the cup, representing Christ's bloodshed for our sins. As we search our hearts, we ask God to forgive our sins, help us forgive those who have hurt or wronged us, and remove anything in our lives that is unlike Him. We must ask God to cleanse our hearts and souls to be aligned with his Holy Spirit daily. The following poems and scriptures helped me examine, purge, and get into good standing with God. I hope they help you as well.

Forgiveness

And when ye stand praying, forgive,
if ye have ought against any: that your
Father also which is in heaven may
forgive you your trespasses.
But if ye do not forgive, neither will your
Father which is in heaven forgive your
trespasses.
Mark 11:25-26 (KJV)

Forgiveness and Healing

Praise the Lord, my soul: all my inmost being, praise his holy name.

Praise the Lord, my soul, and forget not all his benefits—

who forgives all your sins and heals all your diseases,

who redeems your life from the pit and crowns you

with love and compassion, who satisfies

your desires with good things so that your

youth is renewed like the eagles.

Psalms 103:1-5 (NIV)

Why me?

Why is my life filled with sadness and disappointments?

Why do I look and feel so different from the others that I see in magazines and on T.V.?

Why do I feel alone and isolated, as if I do not belong?

Why do others call me names, put me down, and say I will be nothing?

Why do I have trouble doing the simplest things others seem to find so easy?

Why me?

What is wrong with me?

Why must I endure so much heartache, shame, and pain?

I heard God say, "I made you, I called you and ordained you

before you were formed in your mother's womb. I have a special plan and purpose for your life."

Why me?

The tears and the pain were all necessary and part of God's ultimate plan

to cleanse me, to prosper me, and to use me for

his glory to bless others like me.

Why me?

The real question is, why not me, and why not you?

Annette Craig-Wilson

Celebrate You!

There is no one like you.

You have gifts that only you can give the world.

You have blessings others can only receive through you.

The Lord designed every detail of who you are.

He looks at you and loves you because you are His unique creation.

Others look at you, and they admire and love you, too, because

they see whom He has made you to be.

Author Unknown

Blessed!

You are special,

You are loved,

You are strong,

You are a champion,

You are YOU-

and the world is blessed to have you in it!

Author Unknown

God saw all that He had made; He said it was very good.

(God does not make errors or junk; your life is no mistake)

Genesis 1:31 (NIV)

Keep me as the apple of your eye; hide me in the shadow of your wings

(We are the apple of God's eye; He takes great pride in us)

Psalm 17:8 (NIV)

You are a chosen people, a royal priesthood, a holy nation, God's special possession, that you

may declare the praises of him who called you
out of darkness into his marvelous light.
(God chose you as His own; He has a unique divine plan and purpose for your life)

1 Peter 2:9 (NIV)

She is clothed with strength and dignity; she
can laugh at the days to come.
She speaks with wisdom, and faithful
instruction is on her tongue.
She watches over the affairs of her household and
does not eat the bread of idleness.
Her children arise and call her blessed;

Her husband also and he praises her:
Many women do noble things, but you surpass
them all.
Charm is deceptive, and beauty is fleeting, but a
woman who fears the Lord is to be praised.
(God calls you a "righteous" woman, not filthy or insignificant)

Proverb 31:25-30 (NIV)

To help answer the question, "Why you?" we can find more answers in the words of one of my favorite contemporary gospel artists, Anthony Brown, and Group TherAPy. The song is titled **"You Are Enough" (God made you Enough; You are Not a ~~Mistake~~).**

The inspiring words of this powerful song go something like this-

Don't let anyone tell you that you are not great or you are not fearfully and wonderfully made, you are special, a designer original.

It does not matter what they say or do, all that matters is how you feel about you, you are amazing the moment you think so.

Don't you dare say it is over until God says it is done, you still have a life to live.

You still have a ways to run, and with each step keep moving forward, and he will be there for everyone and whatever you do, don't forget, you have enough,

God gave you enough, you are enough, and you will get through this.

You have enough,

God gave you enough,

You are enough and

you will get through this!

Now Personalize it,

Say It out Loud,

I am Enough!

I am Enough!

I am Enough!

Chapter 6

Nuggets for the Future

*Be strong and courageous.
Do not be frightened, and
do not be dismayed, for
the Lord your God
is with you wherever you go. Joshua
1:9 (ESV)*

Progression Stage

"Not A Mistake"
Two people united for one night

Passion, lust, and acts of love

Conception was inevitable

No birth control or precautions taken

Hard labor, pain, and thoughts of the future

Months later, no more hiding; welcome the new arrival

More like Mom or Dad, who knows?

It is too soon to tell or even care

Look at that precious little face

Full of innocence, love, and potential

There are no thoughts of regret right now

The events and emotions of yesterday have passed

Prayers and thoughts are toward the future now

God, please watch over this precious child

Let me live to see her grow up big and strong

Guide, lead, and protect her always

Use her for your glory

No, she is no mistake, not at all

She is beautiful and perfectly flawed

She is part of God's purpose and divine plan

Annette Craig-Wilson

I was an adult when I finally realized my life was not a horrible mistake. Today, I boldly proclaim that I am not a mistake, and neither are you. We were all created for significance and as part of God's purpose and divine plan. God does not haphazardly create or make things; he is intentional. His words create and inspire life. In the first chapter of Genesis, God spoke the world and everything around us into existence. In John 1:1, we find that "in the beginning was the Word, the Word was with God, and the Word was God." We were created a little bit lower than the angels in the image of Christ; we were crowned with glory and honor (Hebrews 2:7).

In the words of Nelson Mandela in his famous inauguration speech, one of our greatest fears is not that we are inadequate but that we are powerful beyond measure. The power and light within us frighten most of us. We often downplay our worth and significance because we don't want the extra attention or focus; we don't want to show off or appear better than others. Humility can be a blessing and a curse at the same time. Humility is downplaying or minimizing your importance, accomplishments, strengths, and gifts to prevent any perception of boasting. It's okay to permit yourself to be great, let your light shine, and be the person God created you to be.

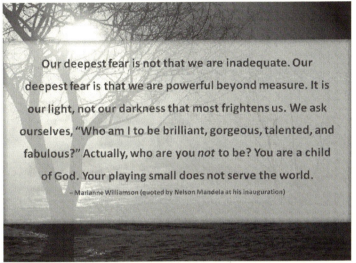

Our deepest fear is not that we are inadequate. Our deepest fear is that we are powerful beyond measure. It is our light, not our darkness that most frightens us. We ask ourselves, "Who am I to be brilliant, gorgeous, talented, and fabulous?" Actually, who are you *not* to be? You are a child of God. Your playing small does not serve the world.
– Marianne Williamson (quoted by Nelson Mandela at his inauguration)

One of the best Ted Talks that I have seen is the **"You Matter Manifesto"** by Angela Maiers.

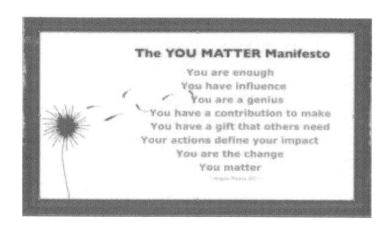

The **YOU MATTER** manifesto is a call to action for all of us to help change our mindsets, those around us, and the world. It challenges us to acknowledge and use the gifts we were blessed with to inspire and empower others to know that they matter in life. This "Mattering" is an ongoing daily process, not isolated.

This manifesto is a deliberate way of thinking, reiterating that knowing we matter is essential to our human existence and happiness. In the world, teenage suicides are escalating, and self-esteem, confidence, and self-worth are closely linked to "likes" and followers on social media. Young people must ascertain that God loves them just the way they are, they were created for a particular purpose, and they matter to their families and the world. This manifesto's major points help us acknowledge our significance by understanding the following:

1. We are Enough

You are enough; God gave you enough; you have been equipped from birth to make a difference in the lives of others and the world. God's grace is sufficient to see us through any situation in life, and his power is perfect in our weakness (2 Corinthians 12:8-9). We don't have to be rich or famous or possess special skills or abilities to make a meaningful difference.

2. We have Influence

It is a tremendous task; however, we can help change the world by contributing our genius to solve the world's problems. One person, like one additional degree of temperature, can make an enormous difference, according to InspireYourPeople.com. At 211 degrees, the water is hot, but at 212 degrees, it boils. With boiling water comes steam. With steam, you can power a train. One extra degree makes all the difference.

3. We are a Masterpiece (Designer Original) Genius is the act of solving a problem in a way no one has solved before. You don't have to have a Ph.D. or a high IQ to be a genius. There is genius in each of us. You must use your insight, creativity, and initiative to find original solutions to problems that matter to the world.

4. We have a Contribution to Make

Your smile and positive presence can bring a big grin to someone's face or brighten their day. Your words can comfort, inspire and empower others. Every heartfelt contribution is essential, no matter how small. Maya Angelou often quoted the old African proverb that "each one must teach one" to help educate our youths. This one-on-one teaching and paying it forward philosophy can significantly contribute to education.

5. We have a Gift to give that Others Need

In first Corinthians 13:13, the scriptures state that three things remain: faith, hope, and love; the greatest is love. Love is the greatest gift you can give to the world. In an often-selfish world, there is a tendency to indulge our gratifications. It is easy to forget that people need positive reassurance to feel loved, noticed, or appreciated, thus empowering them to make a more positive contribution to the world.

6. We are the change we Seek

The change we want to see in the world begins with us. Every little encounter with others helps us realize we matter because we can choose to make others feel better about themselves and their life. A shared smile, encouraging words, or acts of kindness can leave a positive and lasting impression on our daily encounters.

7. Our Actions define our Impact

James 2:17 tells us that faith without works is dead or meaningless. Action is the world's greatest asset or advantage. We don't need to wait until we have more time or money to tell someone they matter.

8. We all MATTER

Many people do not grow up feeling they matter; the world does not constantly affirm this notion or show them that they matter. You can make others feel significant by saying, "You matter." To matter means to be of consequence or importance to others. It means something is substantial, relevant, worthy of note, and valuable.

The fact is that each of us does matter; our life has a purpose, meaning, and value; that's why God created us. We can help others recognize their worth by acknowledging or noticing them, their contributions, and their unique God-given gifts and talents. We can help inspire and empower others to improve and be better by showing them that we believe in and trust them. We can let others know we have confidence in their abilities to create and accomplish great work.

Despite what others say or do to the contrary, we are all significant. The world needs each of us and the unique gifts placed within us. We are blessed to be a blessing to others. We must start each day with a grateful attitude and remind ourselves that we matter. The best answer to the question of "Why me and why you" is because" We Matter" and "We are not a Mistake!"

Be intentional about letting others know:

I see you

I believe in you

You have potential

You make a difference

You can do anything that you make up

your mind to do

You were created for great things

You can change the world for the better

Daily Positive Affirmations
(I remind myself daily of whom God created me to be)

Why Me …because I AM

Anointed

Blessed

Chosen

Loved

Beautiful

Special

Compassionate

Healthy

Intelligent

Powerful

Strong

Victorious

Why Me… because that's the way God created Me!

My life is Not a ~~Mistake~~.

I am Anointed, Blessed, and Chosen by God.

Chapter 7

Growth and New Opportunities

*Each one should test their actions.
Then they can take pride in themselves alone,
without comparing themselves to someone else,
for each one should carry their own load.
Nevertheless, the one who receives instruction in
the Word should share
all good things with their instructor.
Do not be deceived:
God cannot be mocked.
A man reaps what he sows. Galatians
6:4-7 (NIV)*

Self-Examination Stage

"Not A Mistake" – Takeaway Study Questions

1. This book resonates with anyone who has felt picked on, discriminated against, different, inferior, deprived, lonely, isolated, ugly, unloved, unwanted, slow, or stupid. If you ever felt this way or were called disparaging and degrading words, then you have probably asked yourself, "Why me?" or "Is my life a mistake?" According to Proverbs 18:21, the tongue has the power of life and death. Our words can hurt and damage and speak good and bad things into existence. **What negative remarks or comments were said about you or caused you to feel unworthy or less than the person God created you to be?**

_____

_____

_____

_____

2. This book helps you understand that everything you are going through now or have endured in the past will eventually work out for your good (Romans 8:28). My mother's old saying is true.

"What does not kill you will make you stronger" (Proverbs 24:16). The key is learning from your mistakes and trials and using the naysayers to motivate you to work even harder to be your best. Please don't do it for them; do it for yourself! **What horrible event or experience have you been through in the past that now you realize God used for your good, to help and bless you, not to harm or destroy you?**

_____

_____

_____

_____

_____

_____

_____

_____

3. This book reminds you that God created you in his image and gave you the power and authority to survive, thrive, and excel in the world. He loves you unconditionally, just as you are, because he created you in his image (Genesis 1:26-27). You are not less than or inferior to anyone else. God promises never to leave or forsake you. He is always with you during the good and especially the bad times. You, dear children, are from God, and you are an overcomer because the one in you is greater than the one in the world (1 John 4:4). **What unique gifts, talents, or special abilities has God equipped you with to make you stand out from others? What were you called to do for God's glory?**

_____

_____

_____

_____

_____

_____

_____

4. If you have ever asked yourself, "Why me?" or "Is my life a mistake?" you now have the answer. The real question is, "Why Not You?" God made you, so he knows everything about you (Jeremiah 1:5). He knew what you would go through and how you would handle it. God knew everything that happened to you would help propel you toward your God-given purpose and destiny. God dispatches special guardian angels to help you, motivate you, and fight on your behalf as needed (Psalms 91:11). Please make sure you do not dismiss or ignore those strangers assigned to pour into you, to help you grow and succeed in life. Do not forget to show hospitality to strangers, for by so doing, some people have shown hospitality to angels without knowing it (Hebrews 13:2). **Who are the people that God has placed as your special guardian angels throughout your life?**

_____

_____

_____

5. How can we show others we notice, value, and believe in them? How did God demonstrate to the world that we needed to acknowledge his son, Jesus, value his sacrifice, and believe in his abilities (Matthew 3:16-17)? The Word lets us know that we matter so much to God that he gave his only son so that whoever believes in him would not perish but have eternal life (John 3:16). It is easy to become jealous of others when they have what we perceive to be more than us. We might covet good looks, more money or material things, more prominent followers or supporters, and more accomplishments or accolades.

However, those who possess those things can still feel lonely, depressed, frustrated, worthless, and insignificant. **Think about your life growing up and the times you may have felt unnoticed and insignificant. What do you wish someone had said or done to make you feel you mattered?**

Appendix 1

Personal Prayer Time

The Lord has done great things for us, and we are filled with joy.
Psalms 126:3 (NIV)
He has done all things well. He makes even the deaf to hear and the mute to speak.
Mark 7:37 (ESV)

As the Holy Spirit moves on your heart, humbly take time right now to reflect on your life, trials, disappointments, heartaches, and ongoing struggles. Thank God for keeping you in the midst of it all for his divine glory. Repent for allowing things and people to sidetrack and deter you from your God-given purpose and destiny. Ask forgiveness for questioning, doubting, and not trusting God in every area of your life. Ask God to cleanse you, create a clean heart, and renew the right spirit within you to do what he has called you to do for his Kingdom. (Use this space below or a separate sheet of paper to allow God to minister to you as you write out your fervent prayer asking for God's help as you reflect on your life and your unique God-given purpose.)

Father God,

Appendix 2

My Daily Affirmations

(Remind yourself daily of whom God created you to be.)

Why Me …… because I AM

I AM _____

I AM _____

I AM _____

I AM _____

I AM _____

I AM _____

I AM _____

I AM _____

I AM _____

I AM _____

Why Me… because that's the way God created Me!

My life is Not a ~~Mistake~~.

"I am Anointed, Blessed, and Chosen by God!"

Self-Reflection:

_____
_____
_____
_____
_____
_____
_____
_____
_____

The End

Let us hold unwaveringly to the hope we profess, for He who promised is faithful.

Hebrews 10:23 (NIV)

Rejoice always, pray continually, give thanks in all circumstances, for this is God's will for you in Christ Jesus.

1 Thessalonians 5:16-18 (NIV)

Meet the Author

Annette Craig-Wilson is the youngest child of ten children. Although she grew up in a large family, she often felt different, alone, and unworthy because God had separated and anointed her with a greater purpose than she could comprehend. Her parents were hard-working tobacco farmers. Her family grew up with little money or material possessions. Still, they had a loving home and all the necessities they needed. Annette is a proud wife, mother, grandmother, professional businesswoman, published author, motivational speaker, certified life coach, mentor, and customer service and leadership trainer. She is a licensed and ordained minister of the gospel.

Annette suffered several disappointments and setbacks while growing up in her rural community. Nevertheless, she never quit or allowed negative opinions or actions to keep her from excelling and pursuing her dreams. As a result, Annette finished high school 10th in her graduating class; she made the Dean's list in college at Old Dominion University. Annette earned a Bachelor of Science degree in Business Administration.

She completed graduate school at Regent University with a Master of Arts in Organizational Leadership with leadership coaching and mentoring concentrations. She is pursuing her Doctorate with Regent University in the School of Business and Leadership. Annette is looking forward to using the illustrious title of Dr. for future published literary works and speaking engagements.

Looking back over her life, Annette realizes that her life was not a mistake. Instead, everything she went through from childhood God allowed to help her grow spiritually, bless others like her and propel her toward her God-given purpose. Today, her personal story continues to unfold and evolve as God elevates her to new levels. Annette is the proud founder and managing director of Craigwil Ministries Incorporated.

Craigwil Ministries is a 501(C) 3 non-profit public charity that offers professional customized services to individuals and families to make their sacred weddings, funerals, dedication ceremonies, and motivational presentations distinctive and memorable for God's glory. Craigwil provides Christian-based life coaching, mentoring, customer service, financial literacy, and leadership development training. In 2019, Craigwil presented an educational scholarship fund that Annette and her siblings created to honor their late parents' life and legacy. The David and Dorothy Craig "Young Pioneer" Scholarship Fund is awarded to deserving high school seniors with a cumulative GPA of 3.0 or greater from rural, low to moderate-income communities. These Young Pioneers are the first in their families to attend college, vocational, or trade school.

To God be All the Glory!

Glory to God in the highest heaven and on earth, peace to those on whom his favor rests.

Luke 2:14 (NIV)

Made in the USA
Middletown, DE
21 March 2024

51383063R00068